THE EI ...
MILLENNIUM
and beyond

from the work of
RUDOLF STEINER

compiled and edited by
Richard Seddon

TEMPLE LODGE
London

First edition 1993
Reprinted 1996

'Lies' reproduced by permission of Penguin Books Ltd.

A catalogue record for this book is available from the British Library

ISBN 0 904693 46 5

Cover by Andrew Morgan

Typeset by DP Photosetting, Aylesbury, Bucks
Printed and bound in Great Britain by
Cromwell Press Limited, Broughton Gifford, Wiltshire

Contents

Lies

Telling lies to the young is wrong.
Proving to them that lies are true is wrong.
Telling them that God's in his heaven
and all's well with the world is wrong.
The young know what you mean. The young are
   people.
Tell them the difficulties can't be counted,
and let them see not only what will be
but see with clarity these present times.
Say obstacles exist they must encounter,
sorrow happens, hardship happens.
The hell with it. Who never knew
the price of happiness will not be happy.
Forgive no error you recognize,
it will repeat itself, increase,
and afterwards our pupils
will not forgive in us what we forgave.

Yevgeny Yevtushenko*

* Translated by R. Milner-Gulland and P. Levi (*Selected Poems*, Penguin Books, 1962).

Foreword

This booklet has arisen in response to a specific question: What did Rudolf Steiner say about the end of this millennium and the beginning of the next?

It is addressed primarily to readers already acquainted with his work, and should be read in the wider context of his book *Occult Science—an Outline*, where a characterization of all specialist terms used here may be found, and of his lectures on *The Apocalypse of St John*, which give a much more extended picture of future evolution. Without a knowledge of what is experienced at the Threshold between the sense world and the spiritual world, misunderstandings are bound to arise.

The booklet is conceived primarily as an index, formed into a mosaic, to the material available for study; it will enable students to follow up through the bibliography any particular aspect in its full context and depth. It would obviously be a mark of superficiality to quote more widely from an index without study of the original sources. The booklet is by no means an end in itself.

The passages were noted in the course of general reading over several decades, and make no claim to be comprehensive. Most are in précis, and only passages in quotation marks are necessarily verbatim. Many passages are not located precisely in time by Rudolf Steiner, and here judgements have been made in drawing them together. No attempt is made to cover the whole anthroposophical path of self-development, on which safe access to the spiritual world depends. A beginning can be found in Rudolf Steiner's own book *Knowledge of the Higher Worlds: How is it Achieved?*

Times have changed enormously since Rudolf Steiner spoke, and quotations from him can be no more than a scaffolding around the development of our own insights. Yet without the work of an initiate, one may not be able to develop much oneself.

We already stand, whether we know it or not, amidst a spiritual battle of immense proportions, between the forces of Christ and the progressive spiritual Hierarchies who guide the spiritual evolution of mankind on one hand, and the powers of materialism and egoism who oppose further evolution on the other. To be forewarned is to be, at least to some extent, forearmed. Only through foreknowledge can we participate effectively in this battle for the benefit of future humanity—of which we ourselves will one day again be part.

Richard Seddon
Michaelmas 1992

1

The Basis of Prediction

Scientists predict many phenomena on the basis of laws known to them in the inorganic realm. But in the organic realm, as in the field of small particles, there are also apparently random phenomena which can only be handled on the basis of probability theory; weather forecasting can speak only in general terms for a short period ahead. In the social field, which is of more direct concern to us, the unpredictability of human individuals is only countered by observation of recent trends and extrapolation into the future; the unreliability of opinion polls is well known, and every businessman knows that new ideas can completely upset his expectations. How then can future society be reliably predicted?

Rudolf Steiner made a deep study not only of the outer events of world history but especially of the stages of evolution of the human mind, as manifest in philosophy, the arts, and in other ways; and this wide background enabled him to perceive acutely the significance and likely outcome of current events. And as a result of destiny and of lifelong rigorous self-development (which he described in the book *Knowledge of the Higher Worlds: How is it Achieved?*) he also became an initiate, with the added capacity to perceive objectively the spiritual world. This enabled him to investigate directly the spiritual laws and rhythms which hold good, as natural laws hold good in the inorganic realm.

The initiate comes to know the spiritual Beings active behind phenomena, both the divine Hierarchies who are already preparing spiritually that which will later descend to become physical event and the powers which oppose them, together with the elemental beings who are their earthly servants both in nature and in the human being: he can see what they are doing (18.6.08*). He discovers that the truly creative Gods have their workplace within the human skin, in the inner organs, and that what permeates these will develop the form of the future (18.7.20). He can see how past phases in the evolution of humanity will emerge again in metamorphosed form during the involution, the respiritualization of the Earth (24.6.08). And he sees too how we all already work with these germinal forces during the depths of sleep, preparing not only our own next incarnation but also the future of the Earth—though only that which is great and cosmic, not the details (27.2.17).

Rudolf Steiner saw further how the destiny lived through by Christ in Palestine will gradually become the destiny of the whole of mankind (7.3.11), and how He planted through Jesus the cosmic seeds, which live hidden

* Lecture reference (see Bibliography on page 51).

in the will of humanity until the time is ripe for their unfolding (6.8.18).

What in this way is growing, becoming, cannot be grasped by narrow conceptions capable of being 'proved'; those are adapted only to what belongs to the past which is already set. Insight into the future has to be grasped by earnest, fundamental and profound concepts, acquired only by effort and activity of soul, which can adapt to the changes in human nature that they seek to understand (7.10.17). Moreover, it should never be supposed that what will happen in the future is already decided if it can be seen in advance—this is no more the case than that an occurrence in the street is decided by what one sees through a window. Foreseeing must be distinguished quite clearly from being foreordained (28.6.07). Human freedom is in no way infringed by it.

The thoughts we receive from spiritual research should become real, practical ideals which actually confer a future on the Earth (31.12.22). These ideals must be rooted as deeply in the spiritual world as natural laws are rooted in the world of nature (C.M.). Knowledge of the future is worthless if it is not changed into deeds, into living impulses of feeling, and into certainty in life (16.8.08). The initiate experiences already the stages of life which humanity as a whole will reach only in the future, and we have to learn from him how to foster the many seeds present within the womb of time which will mould humanity in the right direction. To set aims in this way means in the highest sense to grasp Christianity esoterically—this is how the author of *The Apocalypse* understood it (17.6.08).

2

Background Considerations

There are three broad aspects from which the events of the immediate future need to be considered.

It is necessary first to grasp that the evolution of the Earth does not continue in a straight line. If it were to do so, as the scientific law of entropy points out, the totality of existing energies would eventually die out in a uniform and sterile condition of warmth, and the whole of evolution would be pointless. The breaching of the ozone layer, destruction of the rain forests, and pollution of air, sea and soil are evidence that the deterioration of the Earth itself has quite recently reached a critical stage. Seen from the spiritual aspect (29.11.18 and 7.12.18), it must be said that the original divine forces under the rulership of the Being known as Jehovah (Jahve), one of the Elohim or Spirits of Form, lost control in the course of the nineteenth century. But Christ brought to Earth at the time of Golgotha the forces of the other six Elohim who together with Jehovah had created man in their own image and breathed into him the living soul. And the first of these forces for the future now starts to become active in those who receive the new Christ impulse mediated by spiritual science.

This may be put in another way (20.12.18). The events of the present time are part of a greater battle behind the scenes between Wisdom—all the forces of the past which have created us under the guidance of Jehovah—and Love, the great forces of the other six Elohim which work creatively into the future. Only through the rhythmic swing of the pendulum between Wisdom and Love, not through sleepy rest, will the future be rightly formed. The Hierarchies intend for us only that to which we contribute from now on in full consciousness; and we have to go through inner soul battles that make us strong. But this is uncomfortable, and people do not want it. So they project outside as external war the battle they should take into themselves and fight on the battlefield of the soul. What is in the book *Knowledge of the Higher Worlds* will enable us to be victorious.

The second aspect is that during the last century the consciousness of mankind as a whole has crossed unconsciously the Threshold that separates the world of nature grasped by the senses from the spiritual world that manifests within the human soul. In consequence, human thinking, feeling and willing are no longer fully coordinated. This shows itself in many ways—for example, in increasing mental illness and the development of psychiatric techniques to handle it; in the increase of heartless terrorism, vandalism and drug-pushing; and in complete contrast the possibility now open of spiritual perception in clear waking consciousness, which was developed so fruitfully by Rudolf

Steiner. Mankind thus enters in this century a sphere where both evil and progressive elements are to be found.

Thirdly, since 1879 human evolution has been under the guidance of Michael as Spirit of the Age. As Ruler of the Cosmic Intelligence, the coordinator of the divine Intelligences in the heavenly bodies, he enables the man who applies his intelligence and reasoning to reports of the spiritual world to grasp this through his understanding. He inspires the will to do so, and also spreads the impulse of cosmopolitanism which is so characteristic of today.

3

The Present Situation

Rudolf Steiner already perceived during the first quarter of this century the forces of degeneration inherent in modern culture. 'The forces that have so far guided human progress will be exhausted by the middle of this century.' (14.12.19) Elsewhere he spoke of 'an acute illness of civilization', of 'a real blind alley which will end in catastrophe, the beginning of the Earth's death', and of 'the moral deluge that will engulf Europe'. Today we can all recognize the truth of these descriptions.

We have to face the conclusion that this state of affairs is the unintended culmination of modern ways of thinking, restricted as they are to the senses and the intellect, which have become increasingly materialistic and blind to the complementary reality of the spirit. 'The fact is that modern scientific thinking can only apprehend the corpse of reality' (20.10.18), namely, that which is dead and can be counted and classified. 'Whenever we introduce natural science into questions of social life, we introduce every time the forces of death.' Later (6.2.20), he went so far as to say that 'everything built up since the first Christian centuries on the foundation of old ideas, old spirituality—including all that has so far been presented as Christianity—is falling apart, and cannot be repaired. Humanity is going downwards because of sheer laziness in thinking and feeling.'

But it is not only thinking that has gone awry. 'Whilst the head busies itself with materialistic thoughts, the metabolic processes influence unconsciously the instincts and passions, bringing them to the highest level of egoism, such that people simply make claims and demands, instead of developing social impulses of fellow feeling.' (6.8.21) This has since become commonplace.

It is not the case that the possibility of help from spiritual Beings has been lacking, but this is now dependent on the cooperative activity of the individual person. 'The doors to the spiritual world now stand open, and the gods will immediately help if we turn to them. But their laws require them to deal with free men, not with puppets.' (14.12.19) In a very important lecture which requires to be studied in full (9.10.18), Steiner describes how throughout this century the Angels, for example, have been seeking to implant three impulses in people before AD 2000, and how these impulses must turn to harm if they are not taken up in the will of the individual. On the one hand, the Angels bring a strong impulse towards brotherhood, based on a deep interest in others and the inability to be happy so long as the other is unhappy; otherwise arises the pernicious misuse of sexuality that rebels against brotherhood—witness the increase today in prostitution, rape, selfishness or terrorism that has no respect for the innocent bystander.

Secondly, they bring recognition of the hidden divinity in each other person, so that every meeting becomes a sacred rite, the sharing of ideas a communion without need of a church; otherwise comes a liking for medicaments that damage health, and the danger of bringing about illness for egoistic purposes or profit—we may think today of the drug barons. Thirdly, they bring the possibility to gain spiritual insight through thinking; or else the unleashing of tremendous mechanical forces, again in the service of egoism—we see this today within the field of electronics and computer technology. Elsewhere (11.4.12), Steiner remarks that 'without new spiritual impulses, technology would not only dominate outer life, but would overpower and numb us, driving out all religious, philosophical, artistic and even ethical interests in the higher sense—men would turn into something like living automata'. Many people are indeed already unwitting slaves of outer material conditions.

In another lecture (30.7.18), Steiner speaks of three currents which in particular have great destructive power. First, Americanism, which seeks to make of the world a physical dwelling with every comfort for an agreeable life. This not only ignores spiritual reality, but produces ever greater fear of it, breaking people's connection with the spirit, which would eventually bring the Earth to an end. Secondly, Catholicism, especially Jesuitism, which spreads beliefs that atrophy the forces through which each individual can regain contact with the spirit, and which reserves spiritual blessing—with its associated power—to its priesthood. And thirdly, Bolshevism, the impulse towards a state based purely on animal, physical socialism. This will yet come to the fore again and again under adverse conditions, and will not easily be mastered.

There are many people today, if still a minority, who recognize and deplore the deterioration in our whole environment in the widest sense, and who bring strong impulses towards a different way of life. And this surging in many souls is most important, because (20.10.18) it is precisely the opportunity to experience disintegration in the environment that will turn the attention of individuals to the creative spiritual forces. For it is only by individual struggle against the descent of civilization that the next stage of evolution, the development of the Spiritual Soul (Consciousness Soul) can be attained, and the present age must provide the opportunity for this. For the basic fact is (5.6.13) that 'a plant cannot give birth to a new plant unless it dies. Anthroposophy must develop as an entirely new seed within us, retaining from the dying part of mankind only what is cosmic, universal. Through Christ's death, quite new forces of life streamed out.'

'Whatever experiences may be our lot, we can look to the future with deep hope and confidence. Just as the crystal develops from substance that has been stirred into turmoil, so can something develop for the future only as an outcome of the mighty changes ahead.' (5.11.05)

4

Lucifer and Ahriman

The profoundest challenge of our age is to grasp with full intensity the polarity between Lucifer and Ahriman, otherwise the Spiritual Soul cannot develop fully (7.12.18). There is in modern consciousness a contrast between God and the Devil, Heaven and Hell; but to strive towards paradise, if he intends to have it forthwith, is just as bad for a person as the opposite. We must recognize that our true nature can be expressed only by the picture of equilibrium—on the one side we are tempted to soar into the fantastic, the ecstatic, the falsely mystical; on the other side is that which drags us down into the prosaic, the arid, and so on (12.12.19). This polarity finds expression in many forms.

Again (24/5.10.15), the Ahrimanic beings—highly intelligent, extraordinarily clever and wise—are active behind the veil of nature, and work at the destruction of the human physical organism. When we enter their world, destruction, hatred or the like arise within us, sensuous urges and impulses are enhanced. They lure men to destroy without any benefit to themselves, and

11

replace thinking by all kinds of powers in the lower organism, especially the impulse to lie. The Luciferic beings, on the other hand, do everything to foster egoism within us, and have a veritable passion for creating, bringing things into existence. If these two beings are not recognized, further evolution will be endangered. We need on the one hand to develop clear, exact thinking in place of superficial phrases—Ahriman will never get hold of the intellect applied to spiritual science. On the other hand we must cease to grovel in the inner life, acting out of temperament or obscure feelings of affiliation to some group, but look instead with love at the deeper connections of life around us. Every thousand years (7.3.14), when the millennium approaches, Lucifer and Ahriman in conjunction are able to make a particularly strong attack on human progress, because things are then pictured too emphatically in terms of space and time.

'Before only a part of the third millennium has elapsed there will be an actual incarnation of Ahriman in the West.' (1.11.19) Mankind must live consciously towards this incarnation amidst a physical life of shocks that cannot be averted, becoming as a result very resourceful, and it is through this that Ahriman's bodily incarnation will be prepared (4.11.19). Western civilization will then scarcely be civilization in the usual sense (27.10.19). However, Steiner is reported to have said later in private conversation that the way things had developed, the incarnation could now occur as early as the end of this century. On the other hand, in view of Michael's conquest of the Dragon, he may yet have the power to defer it until the end of the Michael age, in the twenty-third century.

When Ahriman does incarnate, he will, if not prevented, establish a great occult school which would make people magically into seers, though prematurely and without the effort otherwise necessary. But the clairvoyance of each person would be different, confusion would prevail, and constant strife would be inevitable. People could survive, but all culture would be overthrown. (15.11.19) It depends on how human beings are prepared, whether they can resist this. Many people will in any case scoff at the whole idea of such an incarnation, which is just one of the means Ahrimanic powers use to hide the reality. It only helps to know the means through which he works. One is the mathematical-mechanistic illusion of the universe held by science. Another is to foment everything that breaks people into small groups, especially the impulse towards nationalism. But his best means of triumph is to believe the half-truth that the Gospels give the whole of Christianity. (27.10.19)

Moreover, people who wish to take over Christ's sphere of influence will actually call this Ahrimanic being 'Christ'. It will be essential to learn to distinguish the true Christ, who will not appear again in the flesh, from this other being. This is a very real battle, not an affair of abstract ideas—a real battle to set another being in the place of Christ for the whole of the rest of the Post-Atlantean epoch, some 6000 years. (18.11.17)

13

5

The Appearing of Christ

The intensification of the forces of reason now possible—for example, the capacity to grasp the living world in thoughts that are equally living, as distinct from the dead thoughts of the intellect—will increasingly enable individuals to perceive Christ as an etheric figure on the astral plane (21.9.11). This is the 'appearing in the clouds' described in the Bible, but not yet the 'revelation' or the 'Second Coming'.

Rudolf Steiner spoke of this momentous event on many occasions, as well as presenting it in his Mystery Drama 'The Portal of Initiation'. In an important lecture of 6.2.17, he tells us that since the year 1909 it has been possible to be very near Christ in quite a different way from before. That part of man which is not of this world must seek with intensity that kingdom which Christ said was not of this world. For Christ is not merely a ruler of men but their brother who, particularly in the near future, wishes to be consulted on all the details of life. Then human souls will not only obtain consolation and strength from Him, but will also receive instruction as to what is to be done. This is only possible if we learn His language. Why do we occupy ourselves with spiritual science? It is as though we were learning the vocabulary through which we may approach the Christ. If we make the mental effort necessary to understand its cosmic secrets, He will draw near to us and guide us.

Before it will be possible to perceive the etheric Christ, we must be able to behold nature with the eyes of the spirit, in the way that spiritual science alone makes possible (28.9.11). Christ will appear only to those who renounce all that spreads falsehood over life, and social problems will only be solved to the extent that the need for His impulse is felt (31.10.20). The more we feel that we are accountable to Christ for everything we do, the more will His etheric form become visible. He then becomes our karmic judge (7.10.11). It will no longer be necessary to prove the existence of Christ, for there will be eyewitnesses to His living presence. [Reports of this already exist.] There may be so much materialism that this clairvoyance is not comprehended, but it will be there. If mankind ignores it, then it will be limited to those who through esoteric training prove ready to rise to it; others will have to wait until another Earth-incarnation. But the momentous thing is that it might be acquired naturally by all men. (25.1.10)

Christ, unlike Jehovah, did not unite with any one nation, but with universal humanity. It is the greatest blasphemy against Him to invoke Him for any need other than that of universal humanity (6.8.18). Into whatever group we bear our ego, even if that group fights another, we must bear the 'Not I, but Christ in me'. This will not work for the forming of groups, but will spread over the whole Earth the glory of humanity as such (9.1.16).

'By a strange paradox, it is through our inner experience of the forces of evil that it will be possible for Christ to appear to us again, as in the past He appeared through the experience of death.' (25.10.18)

6

The End of the Century

'The momentous tendency of this age is not clearly recognized, we are standing at a most important moment of our evolution, in which preparation is made for the abolition of the soul . . . According to Marxism, soul impulses are no longer worth considering, the forces that drive history forward are material—the struggle for material well-being . . . Natural science holds that the body alone is real, and everything of a soul nature is but a superstructure . . . Before very long laws will be passed equivalent to a declaration that all who speak seriously of the soul are not right in their minds. [This occurred in the former Soviet Union.] Christianity will have to set itself against the abolition of the soul, but it will succeed in this. For it is in the period of bitterest opposition that Christianity will develop its greatest power. Power will be evoked through resisting the attempt to abolish soul, which will force once more the recognition of spirit.' (22.3.17)

Lucifer and Ahriman have the special ability to misuse the name of Christ, so that men who no longer have any

17

trace of true Christianity in them will call themselves Christians. They will specially rage against those who follow the living, progressive Christ impulses according to the words: 'I am with you for all time, unto the end of the world.' (7.3.14) Time and again opposition will arise from those who adhere to the old ways—churches and masonic or similar societies are the natural opponents of what is new. The wave of evolution will overwhelm those who oppose it, although meanwhile they can cause much harm. (20.12.18)

Human beings face a great crisis—either they see civilization go down into the abyss, or they raise it by spirituality in the sense of the Archangel Michael. The anthroposophical movement is called on to appear in nearly all its souls, for the spiritual powers reckon for the salvation of the Earth on what it can do. (16.9.24) Whether those who in 1923 stood with full intensity in the anthroposophical movement, and those who were leaders in the School of Chartres, are able to descend again and unite for the respiritualizing of culture depends very specially on whether anthroposophers can cultivate anthroposophy with the right devotion (18.7.24). Their karma will be harder to experience than that of other men, yet if they try to pass it by in a comfortable way it will take vengeance in physical illness, accident or the like (3.8.24). However, only when the spirituality which seeks to flow through this movement unites with other streams will Michael find the impulse which will unite him once more with the Intelligence which has grown earthly, but in truth still belongs to him (28.7.24).

Spiritual Beings look with happiness and recognition at

the thoughts which we form about their world. They then give us the capacity to form a judgement about the authorities, about what for example is done by physicians in public life. When we have to confront the authorities we need the help of these Beings, and it will be to our advantage to know this, and consciously to receive it. (10.10.16) The words of Mark xii are directly applicable to the present time: 'When they shall deliver you up, take no thought beforehand what ye shall speak, neither premeditate, but whatsoever shall be given you in that hour, that speak ye; for it is not ye that speak, but the Holy Spirit.' Whenever we proclaim Christ with inner understanding, intense antipathy will be displayed by those who instinctively avoid spiritual science. Important spiritual facts will be regarded as fantastic nonsense by the greater part of humanity. And again from St Mark we should draw the strength to stand firm: 'For in those days shall be affliction such as was not from the beginning of creation, neither shall be again . . . And except the Lord had shortened the days, no flesh (i.e. spiritual nourishment) should be saved . . . And if any man say, Lo, here is Christ, believe him not; for false Christs shall arise and show wonders to seduce if possible even the elect. But take ye heed!' (7.3.11)

Events will inevitably involve the disappearance of much that people value and enjoy—a very disagreeable awakening is in store for those who prefer to sleep comfortably (31.10.20). People will be taken by surprise, though they do not believe it, and will be obliged to part with much (6.8.18). Many disappointments await all efforts to direct things into the right path; we can only do

19

what has to be done, often without gratifying results, like fish spawn cast upon the waters, that a few may survive (6.11.17). What we grasp in spirit and determine to do in spirit cannot be shaken, no matter how chaotic everything looks; that will show itself to be the right thing (6.8.18). But if we allow things to take their course, we shall face the war of all against all at the end of the twentieth century (6.8.21).

The world will give us very little physically, even the body will be less healthy. We shall have to take a grip on ourselves and resolve to turn towards the spirit. It was after all not Lucifer or Ahriman who drove man out of paradise, but Jehovah. Now we are to learn through misfortune to turn to the spirit—such is the language that Christ guides us to speak. Men were so infamous as to nail to the Cross the greatest Being who ever appeared on Earth, yet that death is the very content of Christianity, our good fortune and abounding strength. So through misfortune too shall we have to seek Christ in His new form. This is no ordinary comfort, but it is perhaps the only comfort worthy of the dignity of mankind. It does not say, do nothing and everything will come to you. Rather does it say, bestir your own forces to find the Divinity speaking and abounding within your soul; then you will find Him in the universe, recognize yourself also as part of the universe, and be able to work in communion with Him. A misfortune is not always merely a misfortune, but can be made the starting point for the achievement of greatness and strength. (21.12.18)

The mood of downfall will become more and more widespread, though in truth one need not speak of downfall. Our own error is responsible for loss of direct knowledge that the spirit is present in the world in which we live. This has brought calamity, and will make the bloodshed of wars more and more terrible, until we bring to expression what actually lives in our ego. The Godhead has come to rest in us, that we ourselves may labour. A new civilization must be brought into being to replace the old—that is our situation. And the Gospel of John states clearly that the creative principle, the primal power of creation, is not the Father but the Logos, who descended to Earth and the Earth knew Him not. (3.6.21)

We shall not have to wait very long now, after which only a certain number of men able to carry over the culture of the present age into the next will be saved (11.11.04). If just a few people can be found to see things as they really are, then the grim times we are about to face will be followed by better times (22.1.17). 'Civilized mankind must either establish the independence of the spiritual life or face collapse—with the inevitable result of an Asiatic influence taking effect in the future.' (2.11.19)

7

Further Aspects of Evil

E vil is increasingly widespread today, and it is the special task of this age to come to terms with it. Evil forces gain ground in gradual stages, so that people at first tend to take them for granted, and only when they are established is their enormity recognized. The battle to bring them into the service of human progress then becomes quite specially arduous. But it is just in this battle that our energy towards the spirit is strengthened; and if these forces of evil are taken hold of and turned to good something tremendous is achieved for humanity. (19.11.17)

On the one hand we must recognize that 'the quality peculiar to the human astral body on Earth is egoism . . . This egoism ceases to have a dark side when the person transfers their feeling and thinking into someone else; it may then protect, cherish and take care of what belongs to it . . . All that has concerned mankind at any time in the whole of its development on Earth must arouse our deepest interest.' (27.3.13) Therefore we should not delude ourselves that it is only a limited number of other people who are evil. Tendencies to evil, evil inclinations are present in everyone, including ourselves—though whether they lead to evil deeds is of course another matter. This is one of the deepest secrets of our time. Their function is to call forth the opposite inclination, to plant the seed to experience spiritual life. (26.10.18)

On the other hand, our human nature is based precisely on the ability to destroy matter utterly, to throw it back into chaos. We all have within us a fiery centre for the destruction of matter in order that spirit may exist within us. When our thoughts penetrate beneath the mirror of memory, they work into that part of the etheric body which forms the basis of growth and will, resulting in a fury of destruction. The age of intellectualism, afraid to look down into our inmost being, dulled the sight of this into unconsciousness. But it is just by plunging consciously into this necessary centre of destruction that the human ego is forged. By pouring into this centre moral and ethical ideals, we gain the power to bring about good. If we do not do so, this centre tends nowadays to break out into our instincts, and to carry destructive impulses into social life. (23/4.9.21)

Little do we realize the effects of modern living. When nature, especially the mineral, is broken down, the elemental beings belonging to the progressive Hierarchies are driven out, and when we then reassemble the material into a machine according to laws thought out with our intellect, we substitute Ahrimanic beings (19.1.15). When we sleep—and our will is always asleep—our ego and astral body are outside the physical, right within all the creakings and jerkings of the machinery

23

around us, which are then brought back on waking into the physical and etheric bodies, as if crushing them to pieces. We cram ourselves with Ahrimanic beings! (28.12.14) Where a workman stands at a machine and sparks fly, elemental beings appear, and the important thing is that they do so rightly (12.11.16).

Again, in every laboratory and workshop, especially where the inventive genius rules, people are led by elemental beings hostile to human welfare (6.10.17). Banking once depended on confidence in an individual, but now capital is no longer managed by a single human being; through the large limited companies, it has freed itself from control by an individual, and controls itself (24.6.08). Shareholding—so widely advocated today—is thus the path to materialism in the financial sphere. And the elemental demonic powers in all products of technology work unobserved in our subconscious (14.11.20). The exploitation of electric forces—for example in information and computing technologies—spreads evil over the Earth in an immense spider's web. And fallen spirits of darkness belonging to the hierarchy of Angels are active in this web, through impulses of race and nationalism—though their approach is so subtle and intimate that people think they are upholding their own personal impulses (4.11.17).

There are Anglo-American circles who cultivate especially those forces which subject the soul to the body and bind it to the Earth. Through sport and similar instinctive but well-directed things, males especially are led to feel the forces of gravity in their legs and hands, as some apes already do. Such circles even aim to cause the cessation of repeated Earth lives, by leading souls to feel akin to the Earth forces, so that after death they live on around the Earth as souls of the dead. Anglo-American spiritual life will in essence descend to future ages through women. (9.7.18)

An occult group even exists which leads people without preparation to a knowledge of the destructive Ahrimanic beings, so that their instincts are aroused to take pleasure not only in destroying things but also in tormenting people (24.10.15).

It is also to be taken seriously that beings who will become man during Jupiter evolution are already making themselves felt. They take possession of human will-power when consciousness is obscured, and act with their own consciousness. This is a problem of great magnitude. They enter the senses through the air, and we can only drive them away if we realize that the senses are permeated by soul-activity (such as we perceive as after-image). Although sub-human, they are controlled by Ahrimanic beings stronger than people who have not developed their souls through spiritual activity. Unless Christ has taken hold of the heart realm they suck in Lucifer, and only the constant activity of Michael arms one against them. (29.11.19)

Yet other beings are beginning to generate evil with a far mightier force than Lucifer and Ahriman. Their lurid glare can be perceived in the dissolute sensuality of great cities. Fragment after fragment of the spirit—not the whole—will be torn out of the ego and irretrievably lost. As time goes on certain people will be blinded to all spiritual awareness, sink into animal instincts and passions, and live like animals. (22.3.09) In the absence of a threefold ordering of society, the Anglo-American world dominion will pour out cultural death and cultural illness over the whole Earth, which are just as much a gift of the Asuras as lies are a gift of Ahriman and self-seeking of Lucifer (15.12.19).

Sorath, the Sun-Demon of the Apocalypse, who around AD 666 worked against comprehension of trans-substantiation by means of Arabism, materialism and all that made man animal, and who around 1332 worked in the extinction of the Templars with their cosmic conception of Christianity, will raise his head again around 1998 as the opponent of the etheric vision of Christ. He will arise in numerous men who are possessed by him, outwardly intensely strong natures, with raving tongues, destructive fury in their emotions, and faces which look outwardly animalized. They will not only mock that which is of a spiritual nature, but fight and thrust it into the slough (date unrecorded). In the mystery of 666, or Sorath, is hidden the secret of black magic. The power by which the Sun-Genius overcomes Sorath is Michael, who has the key to the abyss and the chain in his hand (29.6.08).

8

The Twenty-first Century

The etheric body will begin to loosen itself from the physical during life in a great number of people. They must inevitably experience the spiritual world, but unless spiritual science enters the whole of civilization they will regard it as phantasy, illusion, and this already manifests in restlessness, neurasthenic conditions and pathological fears. (13.4.08) Bodies are dying, withering and becoming brittle, and the soul's task is no longer fully to permeate them, but to extricate itself and hover above. Nothing, however, remains empty. As souls withdraw, the body is in danger of being filled by demonic powers, so that we no longer know with whom we are dealing. (7.10.17) Clairvoyance will certainly appear, even during the twentieth century, but materialism may stamp it out, crushing underfoot the budding young shoots. It will depend on mankind whether it turns out to be a blessing or a curse (6.3.10).

We are approaching conscious experience of the Guardian of the Threshold, hitherto undergone unconsciously; though due to a counter-instinct of fear many would rather flee from it. Three things must be known. First, we must recognize the destructive forces of death in our brain and nervous system, despite the fact that we prefer to build and build. Secondly, we can no longer stand fast on views, ideas and opinions that just come to us, but must learn to stand at the edge of the abyss and feel its void. And thirdly, we must probe all forces of egoism, and actually cross the abyss of selfishness, despite the fear. For love, the social warmth of the future, arises only as a counterpart to self-love, and there is no other way of entering the new age than by a true love and interest in other people, felt as a burning fire. (13.12.18)

Our subconscious is invariably taken possession of by the Double from birth until shortly before death. The various Earth forces exert a special influence on this, working into the geographical and racial varieties of mankind (18.11.17). This Double is a great part of the etheric body, filled with self-seeking elements, to which Ahriman gives form. Lucifer too can ensoul a great part of the etheric body with unredeemed karma, so that it appears as an objective entity. In future everyone will be urged by this Double, especially in childhood, to think materialistic thoughts. The ego must learn that it is a citizen not only of the body but also of the spiritual world. (30.8.13) It is precisely the freedom of the human mind that is opposed by this Double, for under its influence it will not be possible to fight against evil, but one will be working against mankind. (19.11.17) Those now given entirely to a material life will in their next incarnation have this being constantly at their side, the untransformed desires of the present life still remaining because of the short time spent in spiritland (27.9.05).

But through esoteric training people will feel that they live in another world, even if shadowy and dim. They will see etheric bodies, at least as shadowy images, with etheric rays and an aura, and will experience the relationship between all profounder events (25.1.10). The forming of mental images already presupposes pushing back an outer resistance by the astral body. But when no such resistance is present, the astral body can push forth two tentacles, the so-called two-petal lotus flower. (26.10.09) Sound judgement and logical thought awaken this organ at the root of the nose. And when we bring this organ into movement, we continually write all our thoughts into the astral light, even when we cannot perceive it. So when we wish to remember, this is no longer a personal concern; the world ether itself calls forth the memory (7.12.19). Only then do we gain knowledge of the true inner life, and we learn to recognize that our real self, our higher 'I', is widely extended over the world around us. The only 'external world' is now our own body. (1.5.13) This is a most important step in human evolution, which needs careful understanding.

Outwardly, vocational life is bound to become increasingly specialized, and people will lose interest and surrender mechanically to it. Life will become so complicated that the machine will give orders to the individual. What we achieve by bodily or mental labour will be increasingly detached from us, and become the point for the incarnation of elemental beings who rise by degrees through Jupiter, Venus and Vulcan. The necessary polarity must be concrete concepts of spiritual worlds. The worker will become united with what is embodied, at first in working up substances into medicines, where subtle pulsations will incorporate themselves into the product. Then it will not be a matter of indifference from whom the medicine is received. And whole factories will work in keeping with the person who directs them. (12.11.16)

A new interest, understanding and sympathy for the environment, which have become increasingly manifest recently, are however a step towards something further. When we rise to spiritual knowledge, the chief thing is no longer the small human being within his own skin, but the whole of humanity connected with the whole Earth. Supersensible knowledge is fundamentally not a relation between what is within our skin and what is outside it, but between what is within the Earth and what is outside it. We identify ourself with the Earth, and strip off everything connected with a particular place, nation or a certain moment. And then we are concerned with the whole year and its seasons, with all places we have been to. When the nature of man becomes a burning question, the urge to understand our connection with the universe will be felt. (6.8.21)

People will increasingly feel themselves as cosmic beings, and out of this conviction—that the cosmos will reveal what cannot come from the Earth—will arise the mood out of which alone the true spiritual Christ will appear to mankind out of remote spiritual depths. We shall have to say 'my kingdom is not of this world', then we can unite with a Being not of this world. If children

30

have been educated rightly, individual souls will emerge from the chaos with a strong sense for the fact that scientific thought has no place for man. The feeling of dependence on heredity—and nationalism is its social counterpart—will become so unbearably oppressive through disgust that a reaction will set in (31.10.20).

In reality Christ has, since the Mystery of Golgotha, become the Spirit of the Earth, and yet He comes from regions beyond the Earth (26.5.08). If we are only stirred by what belongs to the Earth, we can never develop our Spirit Self. We lay the first seeds for this when we Christianize science, for it is Christ who brings the forces we need from outside the Earth. (22.11.20) Progressive Angels in whom the power of Christ is working will teach that the substance of the world, even to the minutest particle, is permeated with the spirit of Christ, and He will be found working in the very 'laws' of chemistry and physics (8.6.11). The Being of Christ will be an object of study, of inner meditation, until one comes to the living experience of 'Not I but Christ in me' (7.3.11). For an increasing number of people, a new all-embracing life of soul will begin from the thirtieth year of life onwards, in which knowledge of Christ—not yet Christ in his full reality—will penetrate them as though through enlightenment (14.10.13). What is significant in this age is that the impulse of the spirit be led right down to grasp the flesh. This will first be possible when spiritual science has a greater earthly foundation, and the spirit enters every deed and finger movement. (13.2.15)

Two new impulses of supreme importance are arising: moral love, and confidence in one another. Great and pure love, much stronger than ever before, will have to be given wings within us; duty will be of no avail for the fulfilment of moral intuitions, the fire of love arising from depths of soul through perception of the deed to be accomplished is just a necessity. We must also meet the other person as an ever-changing riddle, who evokes confidence in an individual way from the deepest depths of our soul. If this confidence is disillusioned, the tragedy of the inevitable distrust will be a deep pain, the bitterest thing in life. (8.10.22)

The Hierarchies have already finished their task for physical man on Earth, and their interest has vanished—that is why genius, for example, no longer arises from the body. We must therefore work on the soul-spiritual nature, and raise ourselves to them, which will restore their interest. (12.9.19) Whereas previous ages all contained some echo of those which preceded them, our age must give birth to a new wisdom that must work prophetically, apocalyptically into the future. This requires the principle of initiation, and it is the task of the anthroposophical movement to supply the seed for this in conjunction with the Christ principle. This summons us to creative work. (5.8.08)

The Spirits of Personality (Archai) now replace the Spirits of Form, who once gave Imaginations to the one who sought them. Everything in the nature of visions is now pathological. We must make Imaginations by our own effort—modern science is the best preparation for this—and then have them verified by the Archai bringing to them Inspirations and Intuitions. (28.12.18) If we truly grasp our spiritual function in the cosmos, we shall feel responsible to the Archai. We shall meet what makes life difficult, but we shall also find everywhere ways out of these difficulties. (18.3.23)

Through external conditions evolution is condemned to materialism: the spirit must be added as free inner deed. The catastrophe of war will return again and again, even in short periods, until people take it as a sign to turn to the spirit. (30.4.18) There will be many a terrible onslaught, and for the most part the purpose will be to continue the war of Lucifer and Ahriman against the impulse of Christ. It is really difficult to speak the whole truth about these things. (9.1.16)

If in the stream of spiritual science there is no deviation from sincerity and purity of intention, it will bring about the right relationship between physical and spiritual worlds. But this involves and demands strenuous effort; laziness in its many forms must be put away. (13.11.17) In those who progress to active thinking, it will be possible to make Inspiration the determining element of soul. This is what Michael rulership really means. Michael does not work so much for the initiate as for those who wish to understand spiritual investigations. (18.5.13) Michael stands cosmically behind man, while within man there is an etheric image that wages the real battle through which we can become free. For it is not Michael himself who wages the battle, but human devotion and the resulting image of Michael (27.9.23). Because Michael won the battle over the Dragon in 1879, the spiritual will lay hold of humanity more and more, and spiritual truth will take root among men, although it will not become the general conviction (20.10.17).

Before the end of the twenty-first century, buildings will arise all over Europe dedicated to spiritual aims, which will be images of our Dornach building with its two domes. This will be the golden age of buildings in which the life of the spirit will flourish. (7.3.14)

9

The New Social Life

B ecause mankind is crossing the threshold at which thinking, feeling and willing become separate, the social basis on which they can do so in a healthy way must be provided by means of an ordering of society which is correspondingly organized in a threefold manner. The basic requirement is for freedom in the spiritual–cultural life—science, art, religion, medicine, education, judiciary and management; equality in the political life and matters of rights and security; and brotherhood in the production and distribution of economic goods. This is a large, complex and highly topical subject, which is beyond any possible presentation here. An introduction may be found in *Towards Social Renewal* by Rudolf Steiner.

It is Central Europe which is called on to understand this, and perhaps if there is no external state and people are obliged to live tragically in chaos there will be the first beginnings of such an understanding (12.1.19). The more oriental Europe becomes, the more it dazes itself as regards spiritual knowledge; the more Anglo-American it becomes, the more it dazes itself as regards the search for the true spirit, the true ego, of humanity. It is called upon to lead humanity safely between these two dangers (30.4.18).

At the basis of all social disharmony lies the fact that machine labour enables spirits of darkness to realize themselves out of the sub-earthly. The lack of spiritual thought about money, credit, labour power, etc.—where the divine is revealed no less than in other realms—is the great evil of the present time. New revelations must go hand in hand with deeper inwardness, which brings inner conflicts (20.12.18). The next stage after the abolition of slavery is that it must become impossible for any man's labour to become a commodity—in future it will only be possible to sell goods or products, whilst people work for others out of brotherhood. This is the crux of the social question, which Christianity must resolve—this very fact will socially bring human salvation. (21.12.18)

Chaos, in which Luciferic and Ahrimanic forces participate, is necessary for human evolution, but is highly antisocial. That is why in the carved group in Dornach the Representative of Man stands between them. In the middle of the nineteenth century Jehovah, who ruled in the blood-stream, ceased to master the opposing spirits, and they acquired special power. In our age the special mission of Christ is to be the Healer of life. At present we do no more than pass one another as spectres: a nice fellow, a good man. What strives towards realization instead is that through heightened interest a picture shall stream forth from the other person, a picture of that special form of balance between Lucifer and Ahriman which he manifests. We shall gain this capacity by paying attention in retrospect to those who have educated, befriended, even injured us—often in a very helpful way. It is here that social impulses arise. (7.12.18)

One who makes a thorough study of artistic forms in painting and sculpture, or of the inner rhythms in music or poetry, who has a deep inner experience of art, can understand the human being in his picture nature in relation to the archetype of humanity. The form of the head, the gait, will awaken inner sympathy and under-standing. We shall only know a person as an ego-being when we see him as a picture of his eternal spiritual being. When we perceive forms, movements and so on artistically as an image of the eternal in the other, we shall gradually feel an inner warmth or coldness—worst of all are those who evoke neither—for the reaction of enhanced interest penetrates our etheric body through the warmth ether. (26.10.18)

The matter of real importance is to grasp that it is necessary for us to become; we cannot rest on what we are. Only when the effort is made not to form judgements but to form pictures shall we take the right path. It will be pictures that will open a path to becoming social. Then only spiritual science is required. (6.12.18)

As a rule we do not encounter anyone we have not met in previous incarnations, and if the Spiritual Soul is to develop as it should what happens between people today needs to play a lesser part than that which works from the previous incarnation. Immediate acquaintance is so impersonal that it cannot be very helpful. What comes from the past takes longer to develop, for it needs to arise as instinctive feelings through rubbing one another into

37

shape, with the help of inner development. It will be increasingly difficult for children and parents, brothers and sisters to understand one another—it is necessary to grow out of the inherited group soul. One thinks that a person should be like this or that; and if they are not, they are condemned. This often obliterates a karmic relationship entirely, which has then to be postponed until the next incarnation, and no progress can be made. Likes and dislikes are great enemies of real social relations. We need to take each person as they are, and make the best of it. (10.10.16)

The task of the Spiritual Soul age, which will only be achieved at its end, is indeed the gradual development of community. The principle of love, which through Christ was born in the individual on the physical plane, now ascends to the soul world to lay hold of a group. (11.11.04) We have in fact only the reflection of our true ego in normal consciousness, but something of it shines in when we meet other people. A person karmically connected with us gives us something real. We are all in fact inwardly hollow, and we should really acknowledge it. If we honestly practise retrospection, we find how much more important are the influences others had on us than what we ourselves allegedly acquired. A person is driven to social intercourse because he is actually real only in someone else. (28.12.18)

Indeed, only when we wake up in the encounter with the soul-spiritual in our fellow men do we begin to develop the first true understanding of the spiritual world itself. The strength to achieve this can be created by implanting spiritual idealism in human communities.

This exists only when we consciously lift what we have seen and understood at an earthly level up to the supersensible ideal level, properly permeated with our will and our thoroughly spiritualized feeling. Where anthroposophy is carried on, a real spiritual Being must be present as a direct result of the way in which ideas are being absorbed, and we must so attune our minds that we can feel such a real Being, invoked by our hearts and souls and attitudes, hovering there above us, looking on and listening. (27.2.23)

Since the 1880s, Beings from Vulcan have been entering Earth existence, bringing the connected body of spiritual science from the spiritual world, and they will gain a foothold if we are imbued with the thought of their existence. People behave very shabbily towards these Beings, by ignoring them; we should understand their language. Their objective is that spiritual science be translated into social behaviour and action. (13.5.21) By turning our hearts towards higher wisdom, we give a dwelling place into which a group soul can incarnate. This ideal was once placed before humanity most powerfully, when men aglow with a common feeling of love and devotion united for a common deed. This harmony of feeling provided for the Holy Spirit, the group soul, to sink into incarnation. When people know what this means, the Whitsun festival of united soul-endeavour will again become alive for them. (7.6.08)

The elements of ferment and increasing diversity come from the past; Spirits leading into the supersensible bring people together. Much will depend on our seeking spiritually in Christ the uniter of the whole of humanity. (9.1.16)

The solutions to social problems must come from across the Threshold; they cannot be deduced from spiritual science (17.1.20).

10

Relationship to the Deceased

We are only separated from the dead through our inability to perceive how their actions play into our life. We live under the illusion that our deeds are ours because they flow from our feelings or will impulses; in reality, deeds flow out of the actions of the departed at every moment that we act. It will be important to grasp with our feeling and will how, when we do something in common with others, we do so in common also with the dead in their association with the Archai. They are embedded in the social, ethical-moral life of an age woven by the Time Spirits as an unceasing stream of universal wisdom and will-activity. We cannot achieve any fruitful work in this sphere unless we realize this. (10.12.17) Only after death does human knowledge mature sufficiently to be applied to social life. The dead know better than we what must happen socially, and we need to listen to them and become instruments to carry out their insights. (16.12.17)

Because of the prevailing disbelief in their existence, the dead are forced instead to haunt the living in their

41

subconscious, and this will manifest increasingly in psychological illness. The therapy will not be individual treatment, but the spread of knowledge of the spiritual world. The moment one draws from the spiritual world one's impulses to action in the physical world, one must reckon with the 'other players'—rightly with every single Angel of every other person concerned. The field is crowded. (13.11.17)

It is simply impossible for effectual, fruitful social ideas to be discovered without paying attention to the Threshold. An image of the human soul and spirit lives in the subconscious, and struggles to rise to consciousness. What obsesses people in the West takes the form of a spectre derived from the time of the Roman Empire, the Latin culture of the fourth age. And in the East there is an oppressive feeling—or its after-effects like a nightmare—made from forces coming from the British–American world dominion, which want to wake people up to see what is really happening. (29.11.18)

11

East and West

The militarization of economics into a great machine, where work is totally separated from the human being, evokes will-demons in whose sphere man is cast adrift (14.11.20). The feelings of the declining upper classes, who want to preserve old customs, confront feelings of hatred amongst the masses. This hatred is the cause of modern infectious diseases—the health of the future depends upon the morality of the present (3.11.05). There was never any possibility that the proletariat fed on Marxism would spread over Europe— economic values are consumed by it, and that leads to nothingness. But we must not forget the Norman–Germanic impulse of heredity, of tribes led by their prince, not only in Britain but also in Russia. (23.11.18)

Intelligence in Russia needs to be awakened, enlightened (whereas in England it is instinctive, and in Central Europe must be trained, educated). Its long suppression to the point of martyrdom, however, preserves it from all instinctive aspects, and this is perhaps the very strength of its development in the future. (15.12.18) The Russians have grasped very little of western religious ideas, but they have felt a great deal, and have experienced in innermost depths something of cultic forms by means of imagery. Mystery cults too were once being preserved (30.4.18), though whether they have survived until today remains to be seen. What is being prepared for the East depends on the German Folk Spirit finding souls who are able consciously to grasp the Christ impulse with their astral bodies over the next thousand years. It would be the greatest misfortune if the East were to injure that which it should cultivate in devotion and friendship. (17.1.15)

Not long after AD 2000, a way of looking at the child as a hidden spiritual being will come from the East. People will ask what might come to light in this child. A sort of cult will be concerned with the growing of a child, with immense reverence for genius. This will work over into Europe, but only influence a smaller portion of mankind. (4.4.16) In Russia and the Asiatic hinterland a brilliantly clear knowledge will evolve of how conception according to certain constellations gives opportunity for either good or evil souls to incarnate—where the blood-stream remains active there will be the capacity to know from cosmic laws and see in detail when to conceive, or not. This will affect morality, with enormous social consequences. Western occultism will endeavour to master the East, in order to benefit from this through intermarriage: the English, India; the Americans, Russia. Otherwise, if mechanistic occultism alone is employed, a soulless population could evolve in the West. The goal of western occultism is to establish a caste of masters and a caste of slaves, from the Rhine eastward all the way to Asia. (1.12.18)

The Far East has a spiritual culture which has wisely been kept secret, and now it acquires western thought-forms. The Japanese form of thought is, as an inheritance, mobile and elastic; and it penetrates to reality. When this unites with the materialism of Europe and America it will undoubtedly gain the upper hand, unless European materialism is equally spiritualized (30.4.18). Yellow mankind preserves an age when the spirit was sought purely outside the physical body. The task of the future sixth age will be to grasp the spirit again in the environment of the physical, more in the elemental world. The transition to this cannot take place without a violent struggle between white and coloured mankind in many regions, which will be foreshadowed in earlier events. We stand here before something colossal. (13.2.15)

Contrary to the western churches, the Chinese—who do not have what we call logic and science—regard humanity as by nature good, and this mighty difference will play a large part in the conflict that will develop between Asiatic and European peoples (10.1.19). The Tibetan or Chinese culture of Central Asia will acquire great significance, and the souls of many pupils of Zarathustra are already incarnated in it. If it flows over the West, it would bring a spirituality in many ways the uncorrupted successor of the old Atlantean culture. (11.4.12)

Whilst carrying out a historically necessary task, Western Europe committed countless acts of injustice against the culture of India and its occult secrets. It bears a weighty karmic debt, and cannot penetrate the secrets of existence without activating this. Tibetan, Indian, even Egyptian initiations want revenge. None of them would ever agree that Christ has reigned at any time in our so-called Christian Europe. (11.4.12) Certain eastern brotherhoods, especially Indian, want in fact to distract attention from Christ. They draw in demonic spirits not belonging to Earth evolution, entice them to clothe themselves in human etheric bodies cast aside at death, and then introduce 'ancestor-worship' of them. (18.11.17) They also use man's lower nature in animal astral form to mislead Eastern Europe from its task of preparing for the sixth age (25.11.17).

12

The Remainder of the Michael Age
(2100–*c.*2200)

During the next few centuries, intelligence will not only be limited to that which is subject to death, but will also understand only what is wrong or illusory, and think out only what is evil, unless it is permeated with the forces of Christ (16.8.19). The levelling out of nation, race and epoch will bring economic strife and individual brutality in power over masses of people, unless morals are ennobled. An American discovery will be how to use magnetism, with its north–south duality, to spread effects entirely in the service of the Double. A method will be found to make the fit ever fitter and fitter by continual 'selection of the fittest', and to use them in direct opposition to the good tendencies of the age. It will become the task of materialistic doctors to drive out the soul by means of a vaccine, if possible immediately after birth, so that the organism cannot come to a conception that soul and spirit exist. And a congress will declare that if a man thinks at all of soul and spirit, that is a pathological symptom. (23.12.04; 25.11.17; 19.11.17; 27.10.17; 7.10.17)

A great problem will be how to place spiritual etheric forces consciously into machines. This too will come, the only question is whether those through whom it comes work for mankind or for selfish ends. The development of consciousness depends on destructive forces, forces of death related to electricity and magnetism. Forces in human nature still unknown will act on these in such a way that people will be able to guide their thoughts and intentions into the machines. (25.11.17) Tremendous mechanical forces will be unleashed in this way in the service of egoism; and people will pride themselves on such aberrations, so that nothing wrong will be perceived. Through mechanistic occultism nine tenths of human labour will be displaced, and every uprising by the dissatisfied masses will be paralysed. On the other hand, there will be machines that can only be set in motion by air vibrations caused by movements which only a man of good disposition will be able to carry out. (1.12.18)

If machines dependent on oscillations were to be constructed on a certain basis, the movements of our planetary system would vibrate together with the earthly system, and everything connected with the working of the stars in the course of the year would be exterminated. Part of our civilization is actually on the way to the terrible degeneracy of resounding to the clatter and rattle of machines and its echo from the cosmos. (20.10.23) But there is no opportunity of ruining anything but the Earth's warmth sphere through intellectual thoughts during the present age (23.3.23).

A capacity of occult hygiene will develop in Central Europe through the insight that forces of illness are only radical transformations of ordinary life-processes, and the healing forces are precisely those transmuted into forces of higher knowledge. No external medicines will then be needed, since illnesses not arising from a karmic cause can be prevented in a psychic way, and karmic illnesses cannot be influenced. (1.12.18)

About the year 2200 a tremendously widespread suppression of thinking will be brought about. From America will come a law, affecting the greater part of mankind, which will not directly say 'thinking is forbidden', but will have the aim and effect of eliminating all individual thinking (4.4.16). When material culture reaches its peak, scorching and exterminating the spirit, one will then come of necessity to what remains in the German people of the healing impulse of Goetheanism, and this will arise in rebellion out of the British people itself (16.11.18). Those who stand firmly in materialism will, however, be quite out of date compared with those who earnestly seek to understand supersensible worlds. A tidal wave from higher worlds is already sweeping into the world. (20.5.13)

Race will gradually disappear entirely, and people will unite instead in intellectual–moral–ethical groupings, while retaining complete freedom and individuality. The Anthroposophical Society is a first example, and the more such associations are formed the sooner the Earth can be spiritualized. Individuals allow their feelings to stream together, and this gives higher Beings the opportunity to work as a new kind of group soul supported on human

49

harmony. If an individual soul keeps aloof too long, it would become a kind of elemental being of quite an evil nature. (1.6.08)

Once people have grown further into reason, the task will be to enliven perception of the streams reaching down from soul and spirit into the body. What streams into the sense organs forms in a natural way Imagination through the eye, Inspiration through the ear, and Intuition through the sense of warmth. Our finer structure is thus transformed to show us how nature actually is. (20.3.20)

There is one fact which we must inscribe daily in our souls, and never forget: in this whole Michael age we have to be *fighters* for the spirit (19.11.17). There is only one book of wisdom, and it cannot come into the hands of Christ unless His followers fight for it by absorbing through their own efforts the contents of spiritual science (15.11.19).

Bibliography

Date	German	English	Page
C.M.	11	*Cosmic Memory*, xi	3
11.11.04	—	Typescript R 73, Planetary and Human Evolution, 13	21, 38
23.12.04	93	Typescript Z 215, Coagulated Electricity	43, 48
27.9.05	93a	*Foundations of Esotericism*, 2	28
3.11.05	"	" " 29	43
5.11.05	"	" " 31	10
28.6.07	100	*Anthroposophical News Sheet*, 1942, p371 (NSL 275)	3
13.4.08	102	*Easter*, 6	27
26.5.08	103	*The Gospel of St John* (Hamburg), 7	31
1.6.08	102	*The Influence of Supersensible Beings upon Man*, 9	50
7.6.08	98	*Ascension and Pentecost*, 5	39
17.6.08	104	*The Apocalypse of St John*, Introduction	3
18.6.08	"	" " 1	2
24.6.08	"	" " 7	2, 24
29.6.08	"	" " 11	26
5.8.08	105	*Universe Earth and Man*, 2	32
16.8.08	"	" " 11	3

51

German references are to the volume in the Collected Edition (*Gesamtausgabe*) published by the *Rudolf Steiner Nachlassverwaltung*, Dornach, Switzerland. Typescript and periodical references refer to the library of the Anthroposophical Society at Rudolf Steiner House, 35 Park Road, London NW1 6XT.